Birthday Crafts

Happy Birthday to you!

make a wish!

by Trudi Strain Trueit • illustrated by Mernie Gallagher-Cole

The Child's World®
childsworld.com

Published by The Child's World®
1980 Lookout Drive • Mankato, MN 56003-1705
800-599-READ • www.childsworld.com

Acknowledgments
The Child's World®: Mary Swensen, Publishing Director
Red Line Editorial: Editorial direction and production
The Design Lab: Design

Photographs ©: Shutterstock Images, 4

ISBN 9781503808157
LCCN 2015958107

Printed in the United States of America
Mankato, MN
June, 2016
PA02298

About the Author
Trudi Strain Trueit has written more than 100 books for children. She worked in a craft store in college. She can build almost anything from craft sticks and glue.

About the Illustrator
Mernie Gallagher-Cole is an artist living in West Chester, Pennsylvania. She has illustrated many books, games, and puzzles for children. She loves crafts and tries to be creative every day.

Table of Contents

Introduction to Birthdays

What is the one thing everyone gets on his or her birthday? Another year older! Birthday **celebrations** go back more than 5,000 years. They began in Egypt. The day a king was crowned was special. He became more than a king. People believed he also became a god. They celebrated this new birth with a party. The Romans were among the first to celebrate birthdays for regular citizens. They

It is common to celebrate birthdays with a cake.

held festivals to celebrate famous people. Birthday cakes also began in Rome, Italy. Cakes were made from wheat flour, olive oil, cheese, and honey.

The United States started celebrating birthdays in the late 1800s. Rich families held big parties for their children. They had cake, gifts, and games. Soon, children from working families were celebrating their birthdays, too. The "Happy Birthday" song was published in a songbook in 1924. It was played on the radio. It was also used in movies. People still sing this song today. People hand made birthday cards. Printed cards became popular during World War II (1939–1945). People sent cards to soldiers overseas. Today, more than half of all greeting cards sold are for birthdays!

Is your birthday coming up? Maybe you are going to a birthday party. Try the projects in this book. Each is perfect to have guests make or to give as a gift. Happy birthday!

Birthday Cake Pop-up Card

Americans buy 3.5 billion birthday cards every year! Handmade cards are **personal**. Pop-up cards are fun to give. They are also easy to make. Treat someone to this birthday surprise!

MATERIALS

- [ ] Two sheets of white card stock paper
- [ ] Ruler
- [ ] Pencil
- [ ] Scissors
- [ ] Colored card stock paper
- [ ] Glue
- [ ] Colored pens

Happy Birthday to you!

make a wish!

STEPS

1. Take one sheet of white card stock. This will be the inside of the card. Fold the paper in half widthwise. Place the card on a table. The fold should face left. The card will open right to left.

2. Make three rectangles on the folded white card stock. These will be cake layers. With a ruler, measure 1.5 inches (3.8 cm) from the top of the card. Draw three sides of a 1-inch (2.5 cm) by 1-inch (2.5 cm) rectangle with a pencil. The fold will be your fourth side.

3. For the second rectangle, measure .5 inches (1.3 cm) below the first rectangle. Draw a rectangle 1.5 inches (3.8 cm) by 1.5 inches (3.8 cm). The fold will be the fourth side.

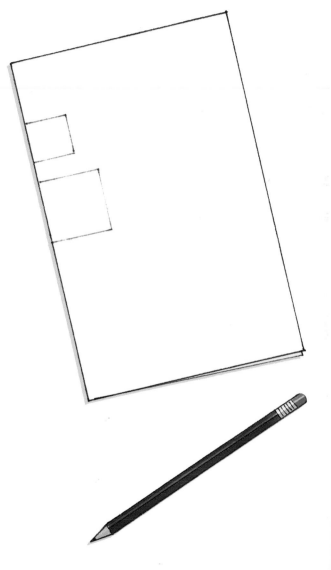

4. For the last rectangle, measure .5 inches (1.3 cm) below the second rectangle. Draw a rectangle 2 inches (5.1) by 2 inches (5.1 cm). Again, the fold will be your fourth side.

5. Turn the card so the fold is closest to you. The opening will now be facing away from you. Cut the two **vertical** lines of each rectangle with a scissors. Do not cut the **horizontal** lines. This will make your cake pop-up.

6. Open your card. Push each rectangle forward. Re-fold the card. Crease the sides of the rectangles. The rectangles will be folded inside the card.

7. Fold the colored sheet of paper widthwise. Glue it to the back of the white card. Do not glue down the pop-ups.

8. Take the other sheet of white card stock. Draw candles on it with colored pens. Cut out the candles. Glue the bottom of each candle to the inside of the top of the cake.

9. Add your greeting. **Decorate** the birthday cake and the card with pens.

You can decorate your pop-up however you would like. Use glue to add glitter. This can be frosting. Make paper flowers or hearts to add to the pop-up. Or decorate the rectangles to look like presents.

Birthstone
Picture Frame

Birthstones date back thousands of years. Legend says a Jewish priest wore a cloth with 12 stones. Each stone stood for a different tribe. In time, people linked the stones to the 12 months of the year. Each stone was thought to have powers. People wore birthstone jewelry to bring love, health, and luck.

MATERIALS

- [ ] 5-inch (13 cm) by 7-inch (18 cm) black, wood picture frame
- [ ] Variety of flat back rhinestones
- [ ] Craft glue

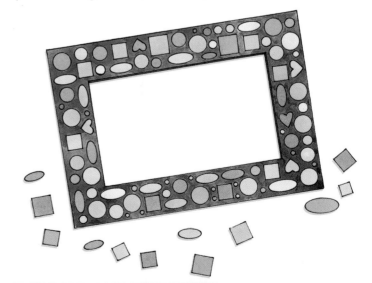

Find the color of your birthstone from this list:

January	**dark red**
February	**purple**
March	light blue
April	clear
May	**dark green**
June	white
July	**red**
August	light green
September	**dark blue**
October	rainbow
November	**light red**
December	sky blue

STEPS

1. Remove the backing and the glass from the picture frame. Set it aside.

2. Choose stones in your birthstone colors using the chart. It will probably take between 30 and 50 stones to cover the frame.

3. Place the stones on the frame. Create any pattern.

4. Dab glue on the back of each stone. Press the stones into place. Glue all the stones onto the frame. Let the glue dry.

5. Insert the glass. Add a photo to the frame. Then replace the backing.

Fortune-teller Jar

Have you ever wondered how making a wish on your birthday began? Germans started the tradition of *kinderfest*. It was a birthday party for a child. The cake had one candle for each year of life. There was also an extra candle called the light of life. Now, we call the extra candle "one to grow on." The child made a secret wish then blew out all the candles. Will your birthday wish come true? Ask the fortune-teller!

MATERIALS

- ☐ 1-inch (2.5 cm) Styrofoam ball
- ☐ Ruler
- ☐ Sheets of colored craft foam
- ☐ Scissors
- ☐ Permanent marker
- ☐ Waterproof craft glue
- ☐ One food jar and lid
- ☐ Tape measure
- ☐ Water
- ☐ Double stick craft tape

STEPS

1. Press the Styrofoam ball to form a cube. Press gently.

2. Measure the sides of the cube with a ruler. Cut out six squares of craft foam using a scissors. The squares should be about the same size as the sides of the cube.

3. Take your permanent marker. Write one reply on each square: yes, no, unsure, you bet, sorry, and ask again.

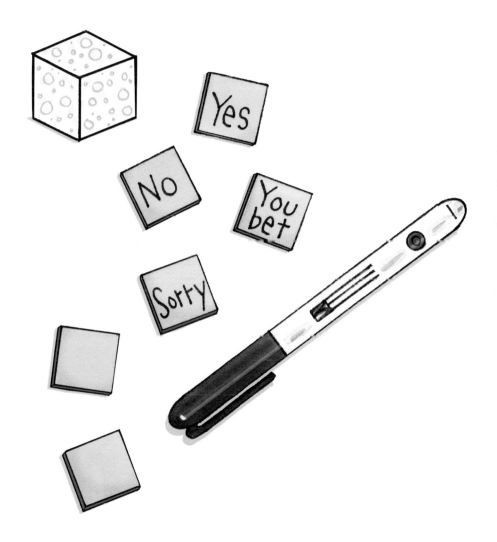

4. Glue one square to each side of the cube.

5. Next, cover the lid of the jar with craft foam. Place the lid on the foam. Trace around the lid. Cut out the foam.

6. Measure the height and circumference of the jar with a tape measure. Include the lid with the craft foam when measuring height. Cut out a rectangle of craft foam the correct size.

7. Fill the jar with water. Add the Styrofoam cube. Screw the lid on tight.

8. Attach the craft foam to the jar using double stick tape. Only the bottom of the jar should be uncovered. Decorate the foam with permanent markers. Cut out craft foam shapes to stick on with tape, too.

9. Your fortune-teller is ready. Ask a question such as "Will my wish come true?" Turn the jar over for the answer!

Wish Jar

What did you wish for on your birthday? Did it come true? Here's a fun party craft. It will get guests thinking about what they want. It may also get them thinking about things they can do to reach some of their goals. Sometimes, even wishes need a little help to come true.

MATERIALS

- ☐ 1 cup (8 oz.) confetti
- ☐ One jelly jar and lid
- ☐ Pad of sticky notes
- ☐ Permanent markers
- ☐ Scissors
- ☐ 1-yard fabric ribbon
- ☐ Beads
- ☐ Masking tape

STEPS

1. Pour half the confetti into a jar.

2. Write down a wish on a sticky note using permanent marker. Maybe you want to learn something. Or maybe you want to make a new friend.

3. Pull the sticky note off the pad. Roll it up. Using a scissors, cut off a piece of ribbon. Tie your note up. Then place it in the jar.

This makes a great gift as a friendship jar. Instead of wishes, write down things you like about your friend. You might write "you tell funny jokes" or "you're a great singer." Your friend will love reading each note.

4. Repeat steps 2 and 3. Make five to seven wishes.

5. Pour the rest of the confetti into the jar. Add beads. Screw on the lid. Gently shake your jar.

6. Place a strip of masking tape on the outside of the jar. Sign and date it with a marker. Put the wish jar where you will see it.

7. Open the jar on your next birthday. Carefully, take out your wishes. Shake out the confetti before lifting each one from the jar. Unroll your wishes. How many of them came true?

Fleece Pillow

When is your birthday? More Americans are born in September than any other month. September 16 is the most common birthdate. The least common is December 25. This fleece pillow is perfect for any birthday.

MATERIALS

- ☐ Solid color fleece, 17 inches (43 cm) by 17 inches (43 cm)
- ☐ Patterned fleece, 17 inches (43 cm) by 17 inches (43 cm)
- ☐ Scissors
- ☐ Ruler
- ☐ Black or dark fabric marker
- ☐ 14-inch (36 cm) by 14-inch (36 cm) pillow form insert

STEPS

1. Lay the solid piece of fleece on top of the patterned piece. Place them so the right sides of the fleece face outward. The right side of fleece is usually a bit bumpy or rough. The wrong side is smooth.

2. Cut both pieces of fleece together. Using the scissors cut out a 2-inch (5.1 cm) by 2-inch (5.1 cm) square from each corner.

3. Using your fabric marker, write your friend's name in the center of the solid color of fleece.

4. To make fringe for the pillow measure 1-inch (2.5 cm) from one corner. Make a cut 2 inches (5.1 cm) up into the fleece. Move another 1-inch (2.5 cm) to the right. Make another 2-inch cut (5.1 cm). Do this around the entire pillow.

5. Tie the fringe. Take one strip from the solid fleece. Take the other from the patterned fleece. Tie them in a double knot. Move to the next pair of strips. Make another knot. Tie the fringe on three sides of the pillow.

6. Stuff the pillow form in the fleece cover. Pull it into all the corners. Tie the fringe for the fourth side.

7. Your pillow is now ready to give!

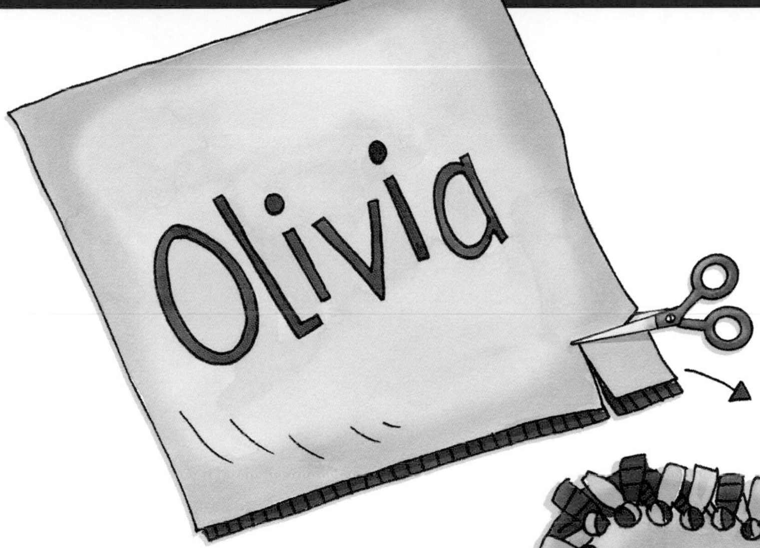
Olivia

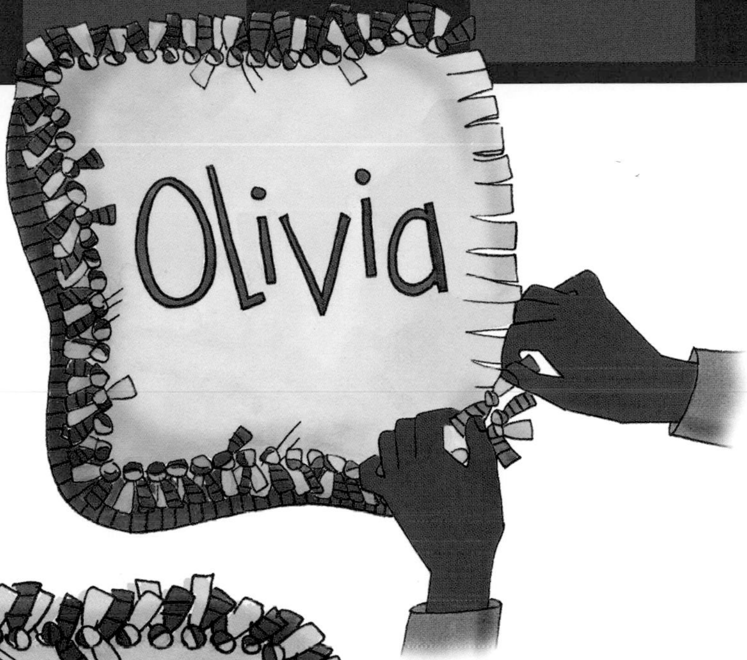
Olivia

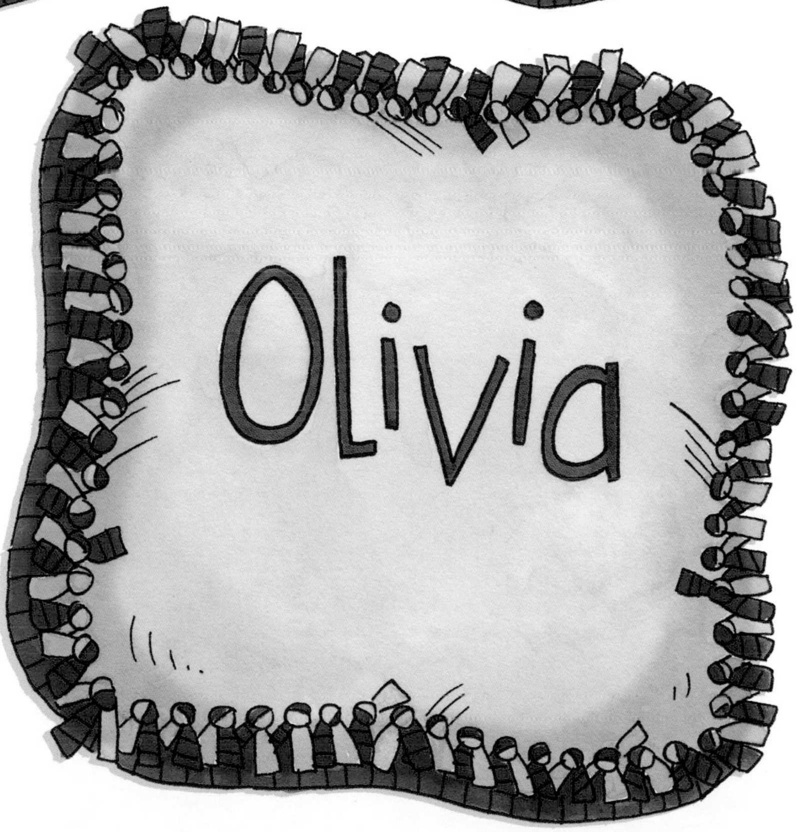
Olivia

Glossary

celebrations (sel-uh-BRAY-shuns) Celebrations are festivities to honor something important. Birthday celebrations started 5,000 years ago.

decorate (DEK-uh-rate) Decorate means to add pretty things to something. Decorate the birthday card with markers.

horizontal (hor-uh-ZON-tuhl) Horizontal means parallel to the ground. A straight line drawn from left to right is horizontal.

personal (PUR-suh-nuhl) Personal means belonging to a specific person. Handmade gifts are more personal.

vertical (VUR-tuh-kuhl) Vertical means going straight up. A straight line drawn up the page is vertical.

To Learn More

IN THE LIBRARY

Berendes, Mary, and Jean Eick. *Birthday Crafts.*
Mankato, MN: Child's World, 2011.

Petelinsek, Kathy. *Crafting with Duct Tape: Even More
Projects.* Ann Arbor, MI: Cherry Lake, 2016.

Speechley, Greta. *Birthday Crafts.* New York: Gareth Stevens, 2010.

ON THE WEB

Visit our Web site for links about Birthday Crafts:
childsworld.com/links

Note to Parents, Teachers, and Librarians:
We routinely verify our Web links to make sure they are safe and active
sites. So encourage your readers to check them out!

Index